I0749792

LEAVING THE SKIN ON THE BEAR

KELLI ALLEN

-POEMS-

C&R Press
Conscious & Responsible

Printed in the United States of America

First Edition
1 2 3 4 5 6 7 8 9

Cover Design by Nicholas Christian
Cover art About Nothing by Eugenia Lolo

ISBN 978-1-949540-31-4
LCCN 2021939665

C&R Press
Conscious & Responsible
crpress.org

For special discounted bulk purchases, please contact:
C&R Press sales@crpress.org
Contact info@crpress.org to book events, readings and author signings.

LEAVING THE SKIN ON THE BEAR

How beautiful you must be
to have been able to lead me
this far with only
the sound of your going away

— W.S. Merwin

TABLE OF CONTENTS

EAST

CENTER

SOUTH

EAST

How beautiful you must be
to have been able to lead me
this far with only
the sound of your going away

— W.S. Merwin

PASSING OBEDIENCE AROUND IN A MOOSE SKULL

The women said, *you can have a daughter.* The women insisted, *there will be a big scene.* The women begged, *don't mention the snakes.*

That's the way it is with problems.

Spreading the blanket over clover changes so little, but ground can be stubborn, often swallowing its own worms back down before the mallards arrive, and sometimes after they offer their eggs as collateral for a meal needed, shared. In the afternoons, the youngest boys let their penises wag against the wind, looking up, watching for large birds. Only mothers can convince such curiosities, such brazen baby men, about shame.

The men said, *temples of fingernails stay clean.* The men boasted, *these big hands break shoulders.* The men hissed, *there is enough in this sack to make two.*

That's the way it is with marriage.

Mating for life is a sentence without bars. Travel to the water glass and see what swims there. You should know by now—bedsides are just gutters for familiar pleasure. In the evenings, the smallest girls string clay beads into nets they will cast over their beds. The smooth roundness teaches the hair to grow slowly, the back to curl and uncurl throughout the short night. Only fathers know how to close their eyes while swimming in such a current.

When the town's sleepers join hands, palms cupping palms, the lot marks one more day in a year—one more chance to listen when the chorus repeats, you can't walk home with an empty belly.

AGREEING TO NOT SAY WHAT THE PAIN MIGHT BE, IS

We start by fleeing disquietude,
evading arguments yet to form
after months of self-certainties
dissolving in met eyes and fingers

squeezing the other's hands less.
Tiny, disappointing pleasures
in these intentional quietings.

Husband, magpie of compromise,
I have fed you into every locket
window of this body. Our way

of living is never mute. Think
of the coalbed you guard, savage
means to hustle heat, dropping
your head from service to shelter.

THESE THINGS INTO THE FIRE

I.

There is a watermelon seed's width left of lunar light.
Her wedding ring, the history of my body's worry,

his salamander-pale pillow. One at a time. Each leaves
my hand and meets a swift disappearance in heat.

The twelve-year-old girl behind my ribs, her boat
responsible for drowning the jury, has trouble

letting her mother's records fall. Her ring is a corral
for horses that will never be tame, those chewing

their front hooves in frustration to escape. We come
back to the field on our own. She led the way toward

pits lined with mouths. Plastic cracks, the lobes
are lit all at once, an explosion of healthy tissue,

clear, thin veins. This ring in my lap, scans a crown
cast in relief above my head. Jackrabbit teeth

stained with her liver's thick yellow. The brain in purple,
a mother's dime-store basement, too many shelves.

II.

We have agreed to so many mailmen dropping
envelopes as our measure against knowing. Collecting

one means knocking the lot under desk or, better yet,
the hearth my father never built and promised to keep.

It is alright to cry out.

When the next pharmacist calls, I pretend to be sleepwalking
with four teaspoons tucked under each arm. Disgrace is the towel

tossed atop every mirror, silver coy swimming further away from
more tests, from deciding who stays awake on the hospital cot tonight.

III.

In this world her name is *Beneath Dark Water*. What else
could I say that would be as true? We draw from

the blue tubbing of a single respirator. My father sketches
a mile around his boyhood pond. I stir ink into tomato skins

peeled for a week's meals and this is not enough a portrait
for any family, for pickers who stand vigil against the one constant

wind that carries our tent too far. My daughter opens a nest
between her fingers. She forgives and I linger, and neither of us

will become crickets left to their singing. There are steps
from a hospital's roof to English gardens. Corridors too narrow

for the processional I would announce to this girl watching me
pack away all evidence. For some other heavenly prosecution.

GO ON ASKING, THEN THROW A SHOE INTO THE FOUR CORNERS

Is anything *just* a rhythm?
The foot's arch
is the same drum
skin no matter what
nests between the legs.

It's our first child who
comes into the tent
when we are bound
in sleep to cover
the smoke hole
with her closed fist.

The seamstress is rarely
as kind as we remember.
She, too, leaves houndstooth
buttons out for the weasels,
hoping they choke, wishing
their teeth off duck eggs
meant for pickling. We need

affirmation that our labors
are bigger than *I saw that*
thing you did. Have you not
realized that the husband
you love has two foxtails
behind his back? How dare
any of us forget how
to spoon dirt into our mouths.

BETWEEN OUR BODIES

We know someone large
is behind us when we reach
our first chubby hand up
toward the sweet thing
we desire to bring
into the mouth,
to feel Eskimo round
and unthreatened,
if just for that instant
past chewing. Size
means age to the very young.

Terrible fear comes later.
Being afraid happens
when the rational ego
steals pudding we set aside
for a luminous aunt, sister
to a mother who slapped
our fat wrists
one too many times.

You see, this flesh
is the same from purple
umbilicious to pubic blossom
to the thin knees surviving
an Appalachian trail walked
a month too long. Sitting
in the bus, the despicable
greed of the child
you were stretches an arm
into your throat, wraps around
that heron-white neck,
chokes you instantly to sleep.

WE MEET AS ROCKS LEFT BEHIND ON THE PLOWED FIELD

Listen to each other suffer. Hold
a hand to fresh wounds, not to push
hard, not to stop what flows. We
are desolate when looking for yellow
milk dripping slow, tipping a swollen belt

of teats under too many teeth hovering
above. Have you memorized how to cure
elk left near a cave's mouth? Epics
tell us how to hold the figs between
our lips, but not how to fall drunk
into clean urban streets before funerals.

This is why bleeding matters to the chalice
kept in every attic window. The mornings
we wake are long mornings. Our belly-
buttons announce arrival after the curtains
are drawn wide, no matter if the concert goes

on without us in the round pit. Misunderstanding
keeps mud churning for when ducks find their way
home and we praise their filthy feathers directly
into our stove. All women know nothing carries
them away from white coals, fingernails bitten
into the thin lines we mistake for a harvest moon.

6893 MILES FROM THE EAR OF THIS DONKEY

A Yarbrough in February is another bucket
of ratoons gone to waste. My China-mother,

full north, collects morning glories, thinks
of horses mud-smeared, and remembers

adding ginger too late for the Shenyang midwives
she feeds before the winter sun swallows magpies

right out of the wind. Woman of my afternoons,
grandmother in the year before oxen, I recite

each phrase you made a mantra, downstairs
early, *Chien Niu* and *Chih Neu* sighed from

the side of your mouth not gripping always
a tiny cigar. Dung dark leaves flecked your lips

and sometimes seasoned the one extra bundle
of fibrous ropes you slipped into my hands.

I would tell you now, Tiger-aunt, story keeper,
that I remain a poor seamstress. I am missing

you now, tucking okra thread into my pockets,
nodding through steam, still looking for rivers.

ROOTS MILK FULL BURST INTO FLOWER AFTER A LONG TIME UNDERNEATH

We resemble pavilions
just under dust. Their slight
roofs are our bellies and I
am tired of being a boy
in his birch tree,
a girl drowning accidental
horses in a rising river.

There are spades trying
to break free under this earth.
What are we to do, possessed
as we are with seeing water
towers fall into tidal pools?
When still a child, I made up
a woman and let her save herself

from my first tower. Lean closer
and we can both hear her climb
the vines back down. Some almost
clear morning you will step
over your boat and the shore
you love will be a road
amounting to eating

despair, to six elements
whose signs are carved willow,
saplings rotating into curl. Every
day we are fifty years old, sitting
down with toast, honey gathered
in black hills, and angry prophets
fill the cupboards behind shoulders.

Oh, we are gorgeous yet, trying
to make placentas into snow globes

for the beloved we forgave, the one
who touched our thighs with eyelashes
as black as gazelle hooves. We are light
when removing the abalone necklace
to cover a tiger's paw. Soon, the pride
comes home and we say "again!"
while lacing our boots, filling
buckets with scallops, waiting
to eat inheritance like fig seeds plucked
quiet from our teeth before the pyre is lit.

NOT THE FIRST TIME TO ENTER TONIGHT

Passwords to enter the washhouse
are tattooed small across elder asses
and we have to bend waists extra low

to catch the fading glyphs humping
along from sulfur springs to nickel-
plated knockers guarding squat doors.

But this is just the story you sell
when you want me on my stomach,
pressed full-bellied into cotton springs.

These are tales cast on lines thrown
far into a past you well know I cannot
resist, will instead open wider, pillow

a pyramid my hips mount, climb. They
say the youngest Greek horsemen knew
best how to ease a nervous mare onto one

longboat by walking her backward, rump
a bouquet of sweaty curling hair, flanks
already soaked through want and seawater.

A DECAPITATED MOON

Means twenty-seven caterpillars
will carry the milk jugs home
tonight. One tongue too many
for dancers filing down the pier.

We have heard older stories
about rough tails wrapped into bows
around the mongoose's narrow thigh.
Ours is a continuation upward, a triplicate
of thrusts, one angry grunt, and everything
new to occupy the kingdom. Appetites

are puncture wounds, too, and no amount
of salt can cure meat past its bone, So,
we swallow as gathered crows, a circle,
near three broken crowns, clipped beaks

already numbered. When the whole town
disappears beneath your river's silt, where
will these steeples point? Every midwife

knows to keep her apron strings undone.
The smallest hands still reach for ties
that keep safe what we bind to this earth.

THE NINTH CIRCLE LEAPS FROM FLORENCE TO CHANGCHUN, OR TEACHING DANTE IN CHINA

This cross, upside down, faces unmoved,
watching carp-eyed as Dis births two men
from and into a time not once relevant

since culture revolted, since the books
met their ash, since the paste made of pages
became the white bottled in hutongs.

What if children rise from the earth? Where
then is the end of this life? These are characters
who cultivate ruin, and no one stops screaming

when the bushels are full. This is the state we
are in. People complain, but not in classrooms
in the East. Every unfolded mesh is a spiritual

newscast under immunity. Elderly men wearing
taffeta are swept as leaves into corners past
street dogs and bamboo prayer beads. Shortage

of compassion is a mirror behind these desks,
where one expression turns from confusion
to knowing to indifference to the daydream

we all recognize in our nineteen-year-old selves,
late for lessons, never for kicking duties
heel over waist down flight after flight

of post-war steps in halls grandfathers smoothed
flat instead of eating the dumplings packed
too quick in the briefest nights, the loneliest dark.

IT'S INSUFFICIENT HOW MANY TAILS TOUCH IN THE DARK

Hold this newt while I walk to the river,
he said. In Iceland, when the uncle dies,
his legs are skinned, trousers are made

from hide, and we take turns placing coins
over his shriveled penis. Blatantly alone
amongst so much raw, the trick remains

stealing away the best silver for your own
waiting crotch—Wealth means dreams
which mean more abundance than rats

running circles through their black new year's
paper nests. The months condemning seeds
to dark pods are over, polar winds encroach

on rotting banana leaves everywhere. Blow
off ungainly headdresses, ringlets, too. Yolks
break better when the skull is luscious only

in its own gleam. There is an island close
for burying necks and livers of unfaithful
roosters keen on theft and brutal rutting.

How far, he said, will you drag that boot
after the swelling breaks your mother's wrist?
Such a long way back from minutes and minutes

of nothing, barrels star-marked with holes,
those pockets bulging with blunt shears,
spools of ochre thread, enough spare change.

COME FROM AWAY

We don't always mean *welcome* when we say
or spell the word. The hog god walks near
the woodcutter in an act against war--

wars being the collective, lapping tongue set
to milk bowls in the evening. The other
otherness marks palm-shaped faces printed
in copper that we trade for yellow leaves.

No time for hunting anymore. Noticing
what requires our attention is a reaching
back toward where the sound came from.

Goat-carts are tributes to perseverance,
if not camaraderie. What a tragedy remembering
the stars are not gods. Look up and past
for new neighbors, finding only the self, still.

We want to interview the hairiest man in the pub.
The neck nods *hello* to the ax and we all gather
in smaller boats to set-out for islands at night.

LEAVING THE WOLF IN THE WOODS AND THE SKIN ON THE BEAR

There are button-faced pigeons
in the ulice again. Seven fires
ride in on Mongol beards, blue
sandstorms close behind. Five
notes until everything burns.

Children insist that St. Mary faces
each direction, stones irritating stones,
guards missing the sun going down
as wagons push their own wheels toward
the cliffs. Often, we just wait, agree

to lower the treble, steal extra wax
for candles passing hands. Optimism
means signing our names in ashy
ledgers anyway. Someone keeps
watch at every gate. If we step out

too soon, turtles beat us to the hearth
and the soup over boils. Greed is
a single arrow past the trumpet
to the throat. Grouse fly past as we
expect, carrying Hejnał, resistance.

Ogar Polski, too, keep their feet tucked
closer to the mud when horses come
visiting, no matter the mettle of man
prematurely hoping to ignite a legend,
to drag sons across cobble leading away.

A THIEF, A NAKEDNESS, A BOAT FAR FROM SHORE

My legs are apart, twin otters
sharing a stone between them.
No longer on the windowsill
of my mother's womb, this body
is not her body. The minnows
we vomit we swallow back down—
These slithering selves too much
under water. Once upon a time
Everything ends—the village,
the woodcutting, the orphans'
hunger, and their fullness, too.

MYTH TALKER, DEER SINGER
—FOR DANIEL DEARDORFF

It's a descent, Danny. The archers only miss
before winter. You have gone into that within
so many times. And now that invincible core
steels the eyes from elk to guide the way
forward. We limp toward the trees
together, between guitar strings you left
on the cabin porch and the two crows
who need materials for their hoary nest.

All the cunning in that universe is a gift
under the skin of what will not heal.
We recognized you coming through
our exiles, not to shame our monstrous
greed, but to lift packages from the floor
to decorate our birthing tables, to witness
our sorry faces when we ask what we missed.

You were iron from the quick, holder against
the keys spilt too soon from outturned pockets.
How could we know then to love you as you
built stone-by-stone these men who would stand
over our beds ensuring limbs could uncurl into sleep?

Danny, the way out meant being weary of hunger
for the whole summer. We all end in a salty mound
of food not good enough for the brown rat's shadow.
This is where those myths have gone. With you.
With the suffering of otherness, looking up.

NOT A SONNET FOR THE TWO-BANDED RICE LIZARD

Tossing coins over that forking tongue
means luck, but not always fortune.

Mangroves to rubbish to back-alley blessings,
the alchemist chants *Tua ngern tua thong.*

This lizard is already at the old woman's door,
a girl's tale through the water recounted.

Riding a typhoon of rusty-naped pitta, young hefe
leads his ruffled gang to safety under the yellow cassia.

Those who open in afternoon know in their spleens
the staggering emptiness of rootless mornings.

Crowded beneath these leaves, giant black squirrels
gather your wealth after his leather shoulders bow.

The monitor is a jester involved in both plays: the marriage
and sixteen hermit crabs making room for the lover's escape.

LOGGERHEADS AND SLEEPERS HOLDING VIGIL

A tortoise is a grandfather and I am an orphan. This wife
with mongoose hips and palm-silk hair. We are each the same
limping tugboat. The shore is so far, and the night long enough

for a round of pinochle. The son beneath the table, belly rolling
a tide of specter waves across tile. Insatiable back, spine hungry
to bend and bend, collects pennies for the brute with the straightest

arrows. Candle burner, mother's milk seller, what have you written
tonight? Binder of contours and birthplaces, I see you. Thatch huts
tight against feet bullying your door to open. There is no more of you

to touch after plundering corn fields at midday. This is the shell
that will bury your skull, wrap your builder's plans in mulberry
silks left in an arribada come Sunday, come low water and high.

POINTING AT A ROCK AND CALLING IT A FISH DOES NOT MAKE IT SO

The monk's waistband
contains a single mourning
spirit. Child and mother grow
lean on bellybutton rice.

On the other mountain, a younger
monk accepts the serpent's pearl,
salt becoming water becoming wine
becoming the message we carve
into abalone. The sleeping lady rests

between seasons.

Believe in cultivating the crop
that will bring threads to weave.
The pestle you dangle below
your belt is meant for more
than a single earthen bowl.

THE RIGHT BASKET FOR PALAD KHIK

Narra cocks line-up in stalagmite order:
first in the fleshy crayfish book, second
as a rifle caught post-fire, head pillow

burst into polished wood. The locals
worship here, wistful for an honorary
member to bend its eye toward waiting

bellies and heavy balls. Seasons long
mean evaporating swallows--quick
as berries down the pelican's gullet.

JUM CLIMBS THE TUALANG TREE

Beware the monkey carrying his razor through the forest. Guard your fishcakes, mind the fire! What comes for Jum is older than the Hantu. There will never be enough meal or ripe papaya to sate these hungers. If he waits, stumbles over his own flat feet, the back of that head might fall clean off, maybe the front, too. Then? Only the eyes on their thin stalks will have any purchase at all. Whose story do you want this to be, anyway?

He counts as he plods. He's heard that when the tualang introduces its yellow crown to the canopy, every honeybee is a debutante for exactly fourteen hours. Then comes smoke and ladders high enough to divide sky from earth. Only a proper storm leaves this wood for homes and nights to sea. If the ax fells these beasts, the hands that swung belong to a dead man within the year.

Jum the winnower, the papa's boy displaced in city sprawl. He is a balladeer, a lover of finch whistle and September frond rhythms. But when Jum sings, his mouth fills with honey or rice and the ooze and spill replaces whatever words he longs to speak. The townswomen come every morning to collect the sweet and grains left of Jum's singing in their huge reed baskets, hoping to sell both at the market, or to trade the lot for a single horned cowfish. It's a wicked trek from brush to concrete. A woman knows to cross her arms and wear rock thrush feathers close to the belly.

Jum allows the songs because of guilt. He ends each day by trying not to think of his four sisters still working the family fish shop near his childhood beach. He pushes dreaming aside to complete the nightly mantra, *I'm sorry, I'm sorry, I'm trying. I will sing to fill the coffers. I will sing to pillow your mangos. I'm sorry.* This morning follows the same as every night and he offers seven minutes to the women, slings his pack over his shoulder, plugs ears with cotton, and meets the first of sixteen hundred and two paces to the bus stop.

Today, Jum will see his mother, will bring her news of the city in the drawing he will lay across her plastic table, and will kiss each sister's broad cheek. All without meeting a single eye, not one glance direct or forward.

The stops are simple and he memorized them in his first days wandering Phuket: Green line, Nag, Yumm, Cave-tom, and then, Khao. An hour's walk through pine and palm tree, hermit crabs making their way south, too. And home.

Blue-crested kingfishers are tangled in a mating hump when he plants his big feet onto the sandy dirt. Jum breathes slow, lets the rutting birds' noise push into his ears as he pockets the cotton for the return ride. He touched a breast once, he remembers, let the round nipple harden under his palm, before pulling his hand back and away so fast it slapped his chest in the recoil. The geckos creeping the walls and ceilings in Kappa's room fled at the slap and Jum cupped his hat over his bulging crotch and made quick for the door.

He watches the violet –blue tails pulse, seconds counted as his middle finger taps his thigh, sighs away what he thinks might be desire, and walks. He walks slower than tamarins blink, than purple squid ink their captures at thirty feet below. Jum walks as a boy possessed by smoke.

Bull flesh leaches its blood too slow for pacification. The cock's comb leaves a crater fit for a bowl and the slick collects there as is has for centuries. There are no wood piles for Aaron in these thatches. This is work for dirty hands, clay-stained hands. Jum recalls these truths in the moments between seeing the tree and recognizing that the sight means responsibility. He did not mean to wander this close and now, too quick, it was too late. The arrow had witnessed his shoe's rhythm and unfurrowed its sharp quills to poke both head and spine from the tree's peeling bark just in time to let the whistle of *how, then, boy?* reach Jum's groundsel thick ears.

The Sleeping Lady expels her ghost just once and the tectonic shifts under her tailbone mean maybe we will be born somewhere, too. Though, Jum thinks, the banana serpent grows from the forehead as tightly coiled as the jade. It's where the skin husk falls that spills your children's future and buries the fickle arrow in one of three trees. Jum has been selected by a lineage he has avoided for nineteen years crawling and scooting over the dirt.

As is understood, he empties his pockets at once, bows at the waist, lets the waxy-hard fluff fall from his head holes, and nods at the iron-tipped ruiner of all days. When the arrow speaks, it is to name its price. Nothing less, not a bucket gap wide enough for the tongue to taste water. *Seems I'm thirsty and have been before. I'll see you at dusk for my filling. Wasting your left arm and your right would make you more than a green stump of a man, no?* While the arrow yawned its tip to let rust mark the agreement, Jum let the pale abacus of his mind decide direction. Paces back to the bus, the wait, the wet-rice words for his sisters if he ever meets their faces after the night collects its bargain.

Hours past and lined with paces backward and then, in closing dark, forward to the canopy, Jum greets the tualang with a honk not unlike the dying cranes wandering the rubber factory at the township edge he considered, before this night, to outline the corpse of his childhood. He places two things on the ground under the hollow-spined eyes of the arrow: an iron vase brimming with mustard seeds, roasted, and a bright green bucket warm from chicken blood not even trying to cool.

How often, when waking and letting the first stretch break a morning's silence, do we think about sentience? Neon lights move faster than we ever will and their insistences are certainly bolder than our own. This is the city against what still grows past its silhouette. This is where Jum suspends himself as he thinks too slow, trying to steam engine ahead —a great-great-great grandmother's promise and a burning, acid-bright desire to be down-cover buried in his studio apartment. Jum wants to be anywhere away from the congealing calf-deep wet and the molar-chipping handfuls of spice soon to muffle his already honey-muzzled voice.

The arrow speaks, the tree lets fall the last of its sequin shades, and somewhere too near the monkey tests his blade against his own snapdragon pink belly. *My tip to the tip and no more or less near the shaft you cradle. Hurry, boy, grain crier, lady footed traveler to nowhere far. This is the last of it, of time, of chance and targets met.*

CENTER

Look, stranger, on this island now
The leaping light for your delight discovers,
Stand stable here
And silent be,
That through the channels of the ear
May wander like a river
The swaying sound of the sea.

— W.H. Auden

EVERY YEAR, AN ONLY CHILD

Why carry sacks for wounding any further?
Homesickness is a row of infants born in a boiling—
too pink, clots in their throats muffling
        any cries for going forward or back.

My sister died
after spending the day in the cattle fields,
riding in my mother's unready womb.
A baby smaller than a second stomach,
she breathed for seven minutes before
deciding the heaviness
        of staying wasn't worth a lung's effort.

My brother died
having never looked up
at the sundial above
the crib. I was a toddler breaking
twigs near the canteen in Frankfurt
before I turned a gaze upward to see,
        and then remember,
        what was hung for him
        and became, instead, mine.

Long brass arms were welded
as a gift for my father, becoming
again a father, in the village
near the army base I so learned to love.
Wishes for honey and beechnuts came
with the smooth, round face
of the dial's outer plate: a mirror moon
        for a son, a son rushing away.

When I was four, there was a food shortage
stretching from town into the wider farms
where my apricots warmed and collected
in baskets to mark exits from train stations

and brick churches. I might have guessed
at hunger, but never met its still face.
    I learned later how many wives
    were ordered to hoard bread
    while their husbands starved.

This same year, my father walked
into my baby brother's room,
the straight bridge of time-telling
hanging bright over the pine crib,
and my father picked-up
the lifeless body of his son.

    Eight-months old and organs all asleep,
    no percussions from heart to tiny throat,
    no milk teeth to break free their gums.
    The son in a hurry to not be held again.

It was a perfect morning to carry
sandbags across the river, to prepare
a rich breakfast for a daughter
and her mother. My father became
despair that would stretch between
    his fingers until every print went dark.
    Oats cooled on their own, currents stilled.

My brother and sister are two faces
of the same sarcophagus. It's enough
to fight forgetting, to take the trains
through town. It's enough
    to remember freckles
    over an infant's tiny chin,
    the forehead sometimes late at night,
    now that my parents are long dead,
    that could be as smooth as my own.

An only escort of what disappears.
An observer tracing stitches across
    the family bible. Today
    is a marvel of what we forget.

EVENTUALLY, KELLI

You've made up stories for too many horses
who only want the tender apples, uncovered,
in your basket. Crossing legs or uncrossing
them never stopped balled-up hotel sheets
from following you all the way home.

Your fingers have made room for subway
poles and weekly parades of ethnic-
less cock. Your life before is a photo
album you'll shelve every night until-

Until the weight of your breasts over-
comes your spine's insistence to keep
reaching for so many blue pages. You know

your knees by their carpet scars. Forking
liver into the cat's mouth does not make
you any less a duchess who is headed
right on past her lifeboat and into waiting
rooms, olive green, still taking reservations.

PULLING MYSELF AWAY FROM RECKLESS

God, you example
of fine ruin, a day
ending, sons wrestling
with their own
sons, none of this
is for you. Lord,
the overflowing
nipples wetting silks,
the shouting wives
at seven am, are not
moaning for you.
Friend, bartender above
the alleyways, old man
with eyebrows of crater
foam, laggards are not
zipping their pants
for you. Adonai,
hoarder under nebulae,
remaker of unfolded grass,
the picnic lain in paper
boats is too rich
for the likes of you.
Master, debt-collector
in the academy halls, deep
snowbank retreating
when blue pike break
their winter fast, none
are swimming frantic
into your ratty robes.

ANTI-BALLAD OF THE EUNUCH BUFFALO

The weighty balls hanging in the men's lodge
will feed no one. The revolver stays in the drawer,

and we place the mask of compassion back
on its hook, turning away, this life, a return.

One day we bend the pear trees too hard against
soil and the harvest is shot, gates rusting shut.

Listening, no one is sure who brought meat torn
quick from haunches, so we agree to eat blind.

It's the same advice when we jump-up behind
any carcass and defend our fear, blunt arrows

making a straight bridge across grass. Bodies
are burnt, fur releases its shriveling ring, loud

and plentiful singeing, uneven percussion meant
for fathers chewing kidneys seasoned with ash.

Young bullfrogs confiscate marbled meat, tuck sinew
behind their saw-teeth, and wait all night for rain.

NO-BEAK CHICKENS (AND OTHER FORGOTTEN DELICACIES)

We are no longer safe in the museum. The boyfriend
stands humiliated, hands across his stomach, trying
to puzzle desire against despair. Carrying tulips, we rush

from Poplar to the clearing pond. The soggy yard
has become a cemetery for statues needing protection
from so much rain. *Dear Foolishness, Have you broken-*

up with your waterwheel just because the koi clogged
the pond? You cannot breed a salamander with a pigeon,
no matter how much you want to hold a feathered tail

between your fingers. Remember the sarcophagus packed
with severed beaks? Can we still daydream about flesh
roasting, heads with no tongues, legs trussed and primly

crossed just like the first time we agreed to take trains
everywhere oceans crept too close? It's enough to forget
freckles embroidered over the hermit's dirty shroud.

Someday, these public stairs will stop disintegrating
and we won't bother carrying the candles at night. Potters
take rooms to hide their clay feet from curators late

for dinner and here we are, thin as bamboo, shuttered
as refugees learning the day's skit in exchange for milk,
in exchange for a chance to mouth anything at all.

ELOPING WITH MR. SPARROWLURE

It's time to admit arrival,
in the country of the world
with the most windows open
for two years, for two falls.

When a woman splints
the elbow of a man come
too late, salmon welcome
bears, both paws over mouths.
The bones might free
themselves from skin
but you are not asleep,
and we die every time

a tiny snake emerges
from the mossy earth to bite.
A boy, who is not our own,
will leap from sky to sky
and no waiting skive will
collect his spine from mollusk
jaws, nor open wider when his
shoulders miss their bridge.

We wash ashore pinching
our cheeks, counting welts.
This worry does not belong
to us lure cast backward, reaching
bay waters unpregnant, only
asking *wait, wait, wait, wait.*

YOUR NAME IS MOUTH AT EACH END, TOO

It's a hidden, lungless stone, this waiting.
Whitebait might be emblematic of an immaturity

you still carry in the bulge of your knees, the way
you swallow after speaking, after nodding in agreement.

Tell me, iron smith, man of coals and grinding,
what did you expect after I took you in, closed

your thin waist with the parenthesis of my thighs?
The reflection between my legs ate you right on up.

We still tell each other into flatness, into a stream
populated with sleeping trout. I am sending you away

with a quilt, a goat's pure stomach, and rough lapis.
The corpse of our longing gets fed after shutting the door.

CLIMB, FALL, SOBER-UP

A wound-dresser is already in the forest, somewhere
achingly green, maybe sleeping in the sticky tree
hollow that still sometimes holds nesting dolls
and eggs, tiny gifts, talismans, objects we know
matter, twin feet in this world and the other.

When you come, under sun, scabs freshly bloomed,
populating your back's nude surface, announcing
what the branches left when you slid their surfaces
from canopy to ground, I hand you a ticket
for the grove and we leave together, closing
each door behind, certain that another Carthage
burns softer the sooner we arrive near any shore at all.

Much easier if travel were enough to cleanse the liver,
to defecate the past and line dry pellets in row after
row to mark the way toward pastures that reappear

when whites turn yellow again. Catgut makes
the best assurances against scars. It may be
a long trip from dumpster to dock to pines' edge.
What will you say when I tell you the truth—
that you have ever been the ship in the bottle?

ONE HUNDRED KNOTS

Swords swallow wheat in the north and every girl learns early how to keep rice grains dry in the pockets of her own skirt. One summer begs that there will be another, yet twenty hours can mound granite into karsts before we rub grains from our eyes as quickly as minutes from *yes* to *please, stay.* But so little stays, and we hoard the mouths at our throat.

There is need here, but the word *need* is wrong. Need is the rain, but there is no rain today, just a picnic in the everyday gloss of lily heads craning against still water. And then, as a sigh, there is no time for sweets melting into the tongue, and no time for counting ants in their round march after sacrifice and duty. Choices are made quicker than breath and both have their consequences. One girl keeps what was left, or she does not. *Breathe in, and breathe out.*

Four parts to a mantra as she collects blanket, reed basket, and dried abalones into the shallow of her chest:
The women agree that they have murdered desire every morning for one hundred and thirty-one years; the roofs sagging over these houses proves as much.

No one asks for the milk to arrive at the breakfast table, and grandmothers hide honey under our beds for the winter, where in snow, everything complains.

Spiders will watch arguments from the furry refuge of their nests, debts collected in full.

Nothing spells shame brighter than teeth-meeting-teeth in a dry kiss gone on too long.

These truths begin each week and, by noon, the sun says what she might to every winged thing brave enough to answer.

This girl, who is no bride, is forging one of two princes in the cabbage folds of her womb.

When she understands that the rabbit has died, she bends to untie her slippers and begins the meticulous work of cradling the ribbons into signs for *girl* and for *boy*. The rough silk crescent and dagger will greet her in the months to come as she passes from basin to hearth. She will make this trek in half circles until her head nestles into dried shoots, her legs arching for expulsion and arrival.

At the washing well, she considers how often she is told to marry a brown bull. She has welcomed too many rods to strike her into flame and is wasted through her want. This is known, and this is the silence that follows her as a painted dog snapping at the elk's rump in spring. The village men insist she let the fleshy button of her ear tear into a new tongue her husband can wield when he begins to sing. But there will be no husband.

Her sister will allow only two trips to the butcher's block and the feast is coming soon, though not for her, not for celebration, but to welcome mourning as the cousin to elation. The hand resting flat on her used thigh reminds the stomach of emptiness and emptying.

Patterns to memorize and spirals to carve into just melding iron. Hedgehogs scatter when her chisel meets its target—they know when to burrow into quills and when to leave the newly born for raptor and asp. These, too, are tasks for the growing, the weft securing what will be carried through cave and into a grotto carved by not-yet kings who knit white bamboo into crowns for the unwanted girls, the July wives. These rivers know each mountain goat by name. Where one leaps to ledge, another drowns and becomes a priestess ever gathering salt and scales.

She feeds her toenails to the crows each quarter moon, yet the rounding continues. Too late for death to mean more than itself and too late to keep mirrors hanging from tree-to-tree along the riverbank.

So instead she sits, legs tucked as cranes beneath her thin hips, and asks the brown waters to listen to her stories, to forgive her the gift she will place into the current soon enough. If she sings now, no one will remember.

She paints a tortoise shell across her widening belly. Each finger collects a thick tip to add swirl and plate to stretching skin. Yellow for the corn mother, grey for the second brother to walk down from the steppes. Kingfishers catch minnows in the bright knife of afternoon and will be back tomorrow, and all tomorrows, and will speak nothing when her boy leads the silver fish to a new kingdom.

REMODELING THE NURSERY

It was not wrong to strip paint, to condemn
a door to whiteness. Many reins caught, comings

and goings. Only a single severed plow horse's
head ever bleached and tied between the frame.

Wood once bluer than boiled eggshells when giving
birth, and planned salamander orange if babies died.

Oils set, bubbled-over splinters, roughing like gills
breathing rust, coughing hinges and fastening nails.

Midwifery begins when the mother's breasts cleave,
a path lain flat, sternum a train run on crepe-thin tides

that we agree to call track. Cheating fathers, drinkers
late to the birth, swindled into thinking they might bundle

one whole life into three clean knots, travel far, always
just past range for the smallest oyster shells to slam tight.

UNCROSSED LEGS, LESSONS ALREADY TOO LATE

A woman holds a mirror to what her grandmother called
a wound. The reflection at 11, again at 20, and before 40.

Years are agile companions to disappointment. Sympathy
for fingers silk hides comes later, too late, maybe not at all.

Our daughters may ask what will hurt, what could fold
to tear. Being a mother means to nod, tilt the chin higher,

scan quick the shelves for stories of agelessness and shells
that stay curled, to meet her eyes, say *aching, too, is just sand.*

Glass cradled between these thighs proves we have nothing
on bless-ed sows, their relentless pride, how much earth framed,
        hours into hours for that one salty crease.

SMOKE, FIRE, WIND, MUD, DARKNESS, AND OLD LIARS

Baking dark bread is only a crime
when the old fireman are left hungry.

Ants will carry crumbs if it rains or not.
Has anyone asked whose diving ball

you are chained to? Maybe it's a good
time to be covered in this much water.

Your hands are never as empty
as your stomach—just imagine

what is carried and where to.
That reckless girl begging for fruit

should not distract you. Pity
is an endless bed stretching down

into the whale's thick gut. Her teeth
are pearls caught in plowed fields, too.

Have you conquered the growling yet?
What can a convicted farmer do

but pull the mule along? Even stag
beetles would catch their pewter feet

in stirrups and tumble off the path
at just the mention of your wild hair.

SOUTH

The excursion is the same when you go looking for your sorrow as when you go looking for your joy.

— Eudora Welty

HOLDING HANDS UNDER THE TABLE

Men and woman living through mudslides understand
a few notions on hiding ancient language. Baby loons

waste their time counting wet tail feathers while lovers
peel damp, body from body, and go on planting begonias

in the one mossy patch agreed upon after blouses loose
their buttons and a grey striped tie becomes wrist tethered.

How easy to mistake a latecomer for a laggard. Grieving,
too, gives passage to the loyal donkey we left tied long

in John's rounding wood. Coming in threes are pillows
for the year ahead, and the one tucking discontent

into parcels for the month's moths is the one closest
to seeing spring bulbs through cotton and mulch.

Who can tell why such sweetness graduates grains to pewter
engraved with your whole name, years noted later, if at all?

PILLOW TALK FOR THE LONG MARRIED

For an elephant to ejaculate
when in captivity, a whole
arm, past the elbow, needs
to be piston-pulsing in
        and out of the bull's rectum,

sometimes for thirteen full
minutes, that cashew gland,
that prostate chapel, requires
a hefty amount of confession,
        of real hand wringing and finger

flexing, for the seminal curl
        and froth to fill a waiting beaker,
        sometimes glass, sometimes thick
        granite carved into an upturned kiss.

SOUTH CAROLINA APOLLO

We know for certain that cobblestones accept heat
whether we gallop toward the hut or not. Loving

a woman means dying every day, too, and one season
begs another to wait just long enough for us to feast

ahead of any funeral. When the Chinese man asks
where are the strong men? and we turn away

to collect fans and ice for approaching night,
does this point to a new August leaping closer

to blindness, to rotten southern fog? The mosquito
swell is a potbelly before our skin ever puckers

back from a bite we expect, ignore, accept as common—
the way wisdom used to be worn as shirtsleeves.

Ponds fill first in June and our poles say Sunday
prayer under willows, un-walled, all hymns cricket

sung and paddleboat timed. We rescue the trial
to relive the moments before. Snows come fast

and there is wet cedar to remind us what muscles need,
where rough hands rest on the narrow waist of our beloved.

GROUNDHOGS AT THE DMV, TESTING THE CURB

We all exhale thick ash when the troll
curled warm in our belly belches lunch,
tucks her knobby arms under her head
and flattens spine-to-spine against space
our mother called *that wicked posture.*

This bitch we carry, the one whose name
has been *Stacey* from the beginning, rides
in the passenger seat of every car we hope
will glide over the roads, windowpane-smooth,
connecting bridge with asphalt that turns
gravel to dirt and ends with a week at some lake
bass stocked and mosquito free.

How is it, then, a wrecked dye job atop
squat forehead and chinless profile signals
means to escape when the convertible door
slips shut and Stacey waits, clipboard pressed
to flapjack breasts, for us to put the metal
beneath the pedal and we just halt, stunned

by our eyelashes in the rearview mirror, by
our wet bottom lip fresh licking an agreement,
by years of hesitation now poured concrete
in our sweaty boot and we cannot move—not
forward or back out of a parking space unmarked,
uneven, and in a town we cannot even name?

The truth is, there are differences between
cave and mountain trolls and childhood lessons
only map marriages and simple diagrams for wart
and flat-ass versus orbital rump. The second us
sleeping until its super is a variety the bestiary
hides in the appendix. Every Stacey roaming
the DMV is one newly born, damp from our own

laze, her fingers cradling the brown score sheets
while our hands, used to guarding stomachs, grip
a steering wheel all over again, the test every-
day repeating, hiding what the seatbelt keeps safe.

WANTING WHAT'S OWED

In the Carolinas, no one seems concerned
that two years just as easily equal twenty.

Grouper turn flat pupils to the same setting
sun from birth to death. People would manage

their anxiousness better if they held their own
crab boxes closer to the stitch where mangrove

roots hump sand. Why is it that we touch
the same bark over and over and still don't

notice ants proceeding down into moss?
Our knuckles have become careless again

and even Elijah leaves the table early after
one glance at our swollen joints. Yesterday

the fishermen agreed to stop crying over rib bones
untouched in the shallows. This far south, the sea

lions are no longer milky white. Everywhere,
what's awake gave up praising decades ago.

THE OTHER WE EAT IS THE TALE WE KNOW BEST

The young girl carries a medicine man
inside her gut, close to the fallible spleen.
She is a healer, a vision-seeker, keeper
of many-colored quetzal and jackal bones
that hop into death song when left tied too long
in leather. Buckskin sometimes rots away
and the girl's stomach becomes populated
with stories meant for the living once
upon that time when smoke shown through
masks traded between grandmas, wild hairs
mapping full circles around loose old breasts.

The young boy carries horses beneath his shoulder
blades, leaning foreheads against a ladder-bent spine.
He is a sweat-slick custodian, a guide toward sand
and flooded caverns that cannot, must not, be traversed
in hours edged close to midnight. Steam and rich-
hooved soil sometimes filters into his waiting lungs
and the boy's breath becomes the tall, brittle grass,
the miles given over to rutting in newly melted snow,
breath that becomes pungent piss collected in bottles
whenever an unbroken mare refuses to hold her heart *still.*

GALLOPING FROM THE HARBOR, CROWN UNDER HOOVES

When a woman leaves Spain behind, every theatre locks
its door and ties key-to-key on a fishing line left to set

rocking in waves for centuries. Today, our two houses
want more to happen and lay the table for wolves

and jackals alike. This is more affections than any of us
deserve and maybe you, too, will remember that hunger.

Some days I am close to death from what I will not drink.
Those tiny bones lining the kitchen window sills remain

an invitation. The sails are hung over our bed now, proofs
solved, or given to some wind we did not ask for. You've
been gesturing for miles for those starlings to follow

you down into the old boat. Don't act surprised when they
crowd the whole stern and you steer right on past this body.

I FEEL EMPATHY AND A DEEP RESONANCE FOR PRE-DEPRESSION ERA SEXISM IN THAT FORK AND SPOON

It takes a swift pinky
and thumb to cradle
an earthworm
home into short grass.

The jawline of the back
steps indicates rot will come
sooner this April
          and *we'll be lucky to pack the waterskins*
          in time for church. These eyelids are prone
          to leather, turning heavy come lesson or lecture.

Storehouses stay dusty the way breasts stay heavy.

Barns are no places for porcelain jugs or delicate
anything. Yet, the wife opens for her husband
and crushes marmalade spread for breakfast,
          all three atop flannel and hay and says
                    weeds don't make for centerpieces
and she rides and rides and rides.

UNCONVENTIONAL FATHERS WELCOME THE ROOSTER AND THE HOG HOME

You and the hedgehog wink four seconds apart
and the fireplace light flickers out. I remind you
both that the cumulative tally of pocketed maps

is two: a brass chain for the one folded, a gold
circlet for the swan-boat made of smeared prosciutto
and mint. Enough treasure to split between spikes.

The way you inspect our hog's pointed toes proves
that between a wolf and Sicilian, we'll never shoot
the dog. This life of ours is a village worth of baby teeth

overflowing the miner's well. Such is the way here,
yearning predicting a molehill's mirth or ire. Skinned
knees mean belly fur stuck again under a long nail,

the one you drag over guitar strings, music a theory
on what timid women need: three windows for looking,
and three for escape. Too many brooms lean light

into these frescos we pretend, and you sweep dust,
so much skin, spine, tiny molars pebbled as mealworms
you roll back and forth, enticement for our boy not yet

aware that he is one counteragent to entropy. Catalogued
hours are thread through a shared bamboo loom. Bonds
ramshackle a propulsion bent on making this, a family.

HERE IS THE WORLD SHE PLAYS:

Hornbill shadows through the threads in her socks and the whole of the lake bundled tight in her belly. Another morning for the girl, another hour watching across shore for her brother's yellow boat. She reminds herself, in this waiting, that what the woodcutter splits is glued over severance when such waters seep wounded skin. This, too, is a duty between daughters and fathers: tending to broken roots before rot's appetite bores holes more than well-deep.

During the month of long nights, a gecko gives its life to the disagreement of two crows. But the girl wraps one thin leg around the other and the nest constructed is no refuge for anything tailed and hungry. It is nearing evening and stretched-out over rabbits, pelts sticky as evaporating nut milk, the mother does not allow agates, cock-shaped and orange-lined, time to speak. The girl listens to the same incantation, the same rhythm, and wishers her mother quiet, just once, just to let locusts sing the dinner dirge. The mother's voice climbs over teeth and tongue anyway: *what the stones say, the river says, too.* This is not poetry for children too many years still ear-wet from the womb.

When the three share a table between them, having agreed to masticate slow, thirty molar thrusts downward each, other breathing creatures align in the way of pilgrims in those woods. Circles form in any space suggested to them—even the catfish looking for warmth curl into one another at the suggestion of a waiting meal. Snails leave gelatin before daylight that the mother weaves into eleven arrow pierced cakes. The father tries not to swallow sand while his daughter's hair collects the baked fletch as she eats, her bites light as an earthworm's lung.

The caution of lilacs dictates a family's scaffold atop grief. Mouths in triplicate give thanks as the mudwork dries and the false gratitude marks success on another floor lain straight and dust cleared. The missing remain so left, tucked behind busy tasks, tidy work to be done day and again. Before unfolding blankets, the daughter, father, and mother reach their arms round the table once more to form a clock. One finger from each hand points to the number for *sleep*, for *when brother comes home*, for *don't forget.*

A NOTE OF THANKS

The work within these paper walls is meant for the students who have come through my doors over the many years I have been fortunate enough to be called Teacher.

Just as beaches, long trails, waters, wells, and caves have offered me classrooms wherein I could play the pupil during my travels, my time behind desk and pen, as editor and sometimes guide, have given me room to be ever the walker between learner and learned.

The prose in this collection comes from the soft nudge of my favorite Pirate and the gentle reminders of my oldest spawn. The tethers connecting image to Story are becoming clearer thanks to these two men who continually gift me their insistence that I believe in my own magic.

ACKNOWLEDGEMENTS

"Roots milk full burst into flower after a long time underneath," "Galloping from the harbor, crown under hooves," and "We meet as rocks left behind on the plowed field" appeared in *Abridged*

"Myth talker, deer singer" and "Groundhogs at the DMV, testing the curb" appeared in *Isacoustic*

"Eventually, Kelli" appeared in *Red Fez*

"A decapitated moon" appeared in *Open: A Journal of Arts and Letters*

"The ninth circle leaps from Florence to Changchun, or Teaching Dante in China" appeared in *Foreign*

"Leaving the Wolf in the Woods and the Skin on the Bear," "Come from Away," "It's Insufficient How Many Tails Touch in the Dark," "Between our bodies," "I feel empathy and a deep resonance," and "6893 miles from the ear of this donkey" appeared in *Eunoia Review*

"One Hundred Knots" and "Here is the world she plays" appeared in *The Blue Nib*

"These things into the fire" appeared in *American Chordata*

"Passing Obedience Around in a Moose Skull" appeared in *Unbroken*

"climb, fall, sober-up" and "The other we eat is the tale we know best" appeared in *Panoply*

"Not a sonnet for the two-banded rice lizard," "Loggerheads and Sleepers Holding Vigil," "Pointing At A Rock And Calling It A Fish Does Not Make It So," and "The right basket for Palad Khik" appeared in *Softblow*

"No-beak Chickens" appeared in *The Stockholm Review*

"South Carolina Apollo" appeared in *Academy of the Heart*

"Jum Climbs the Tualang Tree" appeared in *Gargoyle*

C&R PRESS POETRY TITLES

How to Kill Yourself Instead of Your Children by Quincy Scott Jones
Lottery of Intimacies by Jonathan Katz
What Feels Like Love by Tom C. Hunley
The Rented Altar by Lauren Berry
Between the Earth and Sky by Eleanor Kedney
What Need Have We for Such as We by Amanda Auerbach
A Family Is a House by Dustin Pearson
The Miracles by Amy Lemmon
Banjo's Inside Coyote by Kelli Allen
Objects in Motion by Jonathan Katz
My Stunt Double by Travis Denton
Lessons in Camoflauge by Martin Ott
Millennial Roost by Dustin Pearson
All My Heroes are Broke by Ariel Francisco
Holdfast by Christian Anton Gerard
Ex Domestica by E.G. Cunningham
Like Lesser Gods by Bruce McEver
Notes from the Negro Side of the Moon by Earl Braggs
Imagine Not Drowning by Kelli Allen
Notes to the Beloved by Michelle Bitting
Free Boat: Collected Lies and Love Poems by John Reed
Les Fauves by Barbara Crooker
Tall as You are Tall Between Them by Annie Christain
The Couple Who Fell to Earth by Michelle Bitting
Notes to the Beloved by Michelle Bitting

www.ingramcontent.com/pod-product-compliance
Lightning Source LLC
LaVergne TN
LVHW051020080826
845145LV00009B/2716

* 9 7 8 1 9 4 9 5 4 0 3 1 4 *